EITHER REFORMIST OR TERRORIST

Abhijit Naskar is the twenty-first century Neuroscientist whose contributions in Cognitive and Behavioral Neuroscience have helped the world tackle the issues of systemic racism, prejudice, hate, extremism, discrimination and biases more effectively. As an untiring advocate of mental health and universal acceptance, he became a beloved best-selling author all over the world with his very first book "The Art of Neuroscience in Everything". With his pioneering ventures into the Neuropsychology of beliefs and biases, he has hugely contributed in the eradication of religious and cultural differences in our world, for which he is popularly hailed as the humanitarian scientist, who takes the human civilization in the path of sweet general harmony.

Either Reformist or Terrorist

If You Are Terror
I Am Your Grandfather

ABHIJIT NASKAR

Also by Abhijit Naskar

The Art of Neuroscience in Everything
Your Own Neuron: A Tour of Your Psychic Brain
The God Parasite: Revelation of Neuroscience
The Spirituality Engine
Love Sutra: The Neuroscientific Manual of Love
Homo: A Brief History of Consciousness
Neurosutra: The Abhijit Naskar Collection
Autobiography of God: Biopsy of A Cognitive Reality
Biopsy of Religions: Neuroanalysis towards Universal
Tolerance
Prescription: Treating India's Soul
What is Mind?
In Search of Divinity: Journey to The Kingdom of Conscience
Love, God & Neurons: Memoir of a scientist who found
himself by getting lost
The Islamophobic Civilization: Voyage of Acceptance
Neurons of Jesus: Mind of A Teacher, Spouse & Thinker
Neurons, Oxygen & Nanak
The Education Decree
Principia Humanitas
The Krishna Cancer
Rowdy Buddha: The First Sapiens
We Are All Black: A Treatise on Racism
The Bengal Tigress: A Treatise on Gender Equality
Either Civilized or Phobic: A Treatise on Homosexuality
Wise Mating: A Treatise on Monogamy
Illusion of Religion: A Treatise on Religious
Fundamentalism
The Film Testament
Human Making is Our Mission: A Treatise on Parenting
I Am The Thread: My Mission
7 Billion Gods: Humans Above All
Lord is My Sheep: Gospel of Human
Morality Absolute
A Push in Perception
Let The Poor Be Your God
Conscience over Nonsense
Saint of The Sapiens
Time to Save Medicine
Fabric of Humanity
Build Bridges not Walls: In the name of Americana
The Constitution of The United Peoples of Earth

Lives to Serve Before I Sleep
When Humans Unite: Making A World Without Borders
All For Acceptance
Monk Meets World
Mission Reality
Citizens of Peace: Beyond The Savagery of Sovereignty
Operation Justice: To Make A Society That Needs No Law
See No Gender
The Gospel of Technology
Every Generation Needs Caretakers: The Gospel of
Patriotism
Aşkanjali: The Sufi Sermon
Mad About Humans: World Maker's Almanac
Revolution Indomable
When Call The People: My World My Responsibility
No Foreigner Only Family
Hurricane Humans: Give me accountability, I'll give you
peace
Ain't Enough to Look Human
Servitude is Sanctitude
Time To End Democracy: The Meritocratic Manifesto
I Vicdansaadet Speaking: No Rest Till The World is Lifted
Boldly Comes Justice: Sentient not Silent
Good Scientist: When Science and Service Combine
Sleepless for Society
Neden Türk: The Gospel of Secularism
Martyr Meets World: To Solve The Hard Problem of
Inhumanity
The Shape of A Human: Our America Their America
When Veins Ignite: Either Integration or Degradation
Heart Force One: Need No Gun to Defend Society
Solo Standing on Guard: Life Before Law
Generation Corazon: Nationalism is Terrorism
Mucize Insan: When The World is Family
Hometown Human: To Live for Soil and Society
Girl Over God: The Novel (Abi Naskar Adventures Book 1)
Gente Mente Adelante: Prejudice Conquered is World
Conquered
Earthquakin' Egalitarian: I Die Everyday So Your Children
Can Live
Giants in Jeans: 100 Sonnets of United Earth
Vatican Virus: The Forbidden Fiction (Abi Naskar
Adventures Book 2)
Karadeniz Chronicle: The Novel (Abi Naskar Adventures

Book 3)
Şehit Sevda Society: Even in Death I Shall Live
Handcrafted Humanity: 100 Sonnets For A Blunderful
World
Mücadele Muhabbet: Gospel of An Unarmed Soldier
Making Britain Civilized: How to Gain Readmission to The
Human Race
Dervish Advaitam: Gospel of Sacred Feminines and Holy
Fathers
Honor He Wrote: 100 Sonnets For Humans Not Vegetables
The Gentalist: There's No Social Work, Only Family Work

DEDICATION

To those accountable civilians of the world who would rather die than compromise their humanity.

CONTENTS

1.   Evolution & World Building
(The Sonnet)

Evolution & World Building
(The Sonnet)

One cell became two,
For being alone is no life.
Then those two became four,
To ease each other's strife.
3 billion years later there are,
Seven billion of us and trillions others.
Now how come we wanna turn back time,
How come we hoard all after selfish desires!
Joy of sharing outshines all other joy,
Caring is the very foundation of life divine.
Divinity means neither magic not mysticism,
It's just a common sense that makes hearts align.
The powers of world-building are all encoded in you.
Bring those codes to life and write the world anew.

2. Tyranny is Failure of Education

Diversity is the world's stronghold, nay - diversity is the world, period. And the world that celebrates diversity is a civilized world, whereas one that rejects diversity and insists on cultural exclusivity - tribal exclusivity that is, is anything but civilized.

This utter denial of diversity in the name of heritage and culture is the fundamental cause behind all the disparities in the world. And here's the interesting part - contrary to popular belief, disparity is not a policy issue, it's an education issue.

Every single trouble that haunts our society till this day and age is the failure of education. Let's take tyranny for example.

To rid this world of tyranny, assassinating a tyrant is not the solution, it only makes them a martyr to their followers. Stand up to them, strip them of their position, then throw 'em in jail. There's nothing more torturous to a megalomaniacal tyrant than rotting behind bars like a two-bit criminal.

Killing a tyrant only postpones tyranny. Focus on building a humane society, so that none of the kids ever winds up a tyrant. We can build the world one kid at a time. We'll raise the society one kid at a time.

Or to put it another way, we can free the world from tyranny, not by killing one tyrant at a time, but by nourishing one kid at a time.

In short, the answer is education.

I am not talking about slave producing education, I am talking about character building education, the kind of education that moulds an infant brain into a whole human being - a being who is nontribal, nonsectarian, undoctrinated and nonjudgmental.

3. When Education Produces Tyrants

The pathetic truth of the matter is, today the aim of education is to build not a whole human being, but the opposite - that is to raise a selfish, competitive, opinionated, boneheaded, sectarian, self-obsessed human imitation - the more competitive the better.

With such retarded education in place to decide the children's destiny we shall never have a world without disparity.

We prepare the kids not just to cater to disparities, but more importantly to be the very soul of disparity. When we raise children as vessels of disparities, it shouldn't come as a surprise that the world is ever-lastingly infested with nothing but disparities.

Good teachers make good citizens. When most teachers themselves are egotistical, materialistic, bigoted snobs, how can the students grow up to be anything else! When teachers and parents alike peddle selfishness and competition to the children they are bound to grow up to be either apathetic or pessimistic nincompoops.

That's why it's the middle and backbenchers who change the world, whereas toppers and front benchers only make good employees.

Because academic toppers are expert in memorizing and regurgitating preexisting answers, they are the least likely practitioners of original thinking. In short, they are least likely to be explorers, discoverers and inventors.

The original thinkers of the world, those who actually bring change, usually come from the not-so-special bunch inside a classroom. I was among such a bunch – an average student who never attracted the attention of any of the so-called teachers - just an average student but with not-so-average curiosity.

In fact, even today I can say without hesitation, I have more questions than answers. As a student I was an idiot, as one of the world's foremost thinkers I am still an idiot. And mark you me, only sage is the idiot.

4. The Accountable Idiot

In a world full of apathetic amateurs the accountable adult is an idiot. In a world full of materialistic morons the one living a simple life is an idiot. In a world of selfishness the unselfish is an idiot. In a world of presumptuous haters the naive lover is an idiot.

People are worried that machines will take over the world and then they'll have no voice any more.

Well - what voice do you have today, despite having a voice!

You are already puppets to your political overlords. You don't think for yourself, you don't feel for yourself, you don't behave for yourself - heck, that's why you have election in the first place - not so you could choose a leader, but so you don't have to take any responsibility.

And you are still worried about machines taking over your lives! Your lives are already taken over, not by mechanical deities but by organic sectarian deities born of the womb of your own indifference. So forget about a fictitious future which may or may not happen and pay attention to the real threat that haunts the society in the present - namely, your own indifference.

To put it simply, in a world where apathy, indifference and complacency are accepted as intelligence and the norm, be an idiot and take responsibility. Take responsibility for your neighborhood, take responsibility for your society, take responsibility for your world - nay, for our world.

5.   Drunk, Insane & Uneducated
(The Sonnet)

18

Drunk, Insane & Uneducated
(The Sonnet)

We live in a world where the sane,
Are more insane than the clinically insane.
Greed and apathy are worse of all ailments,
They make a society narrow and vain.
We live in a world where the educated,
Are more ignorant than the uneducated.
Arrogance and egotism are sacrilege of education,
They make a savage out of the most learned.
We live in a world where the sober,
Are more drunk than a sick alcoholic.
Coldness makes vegetable out of a human,
Then they cuss accountability as idealistic.
I'm drunk and insane, with no education whatsoever.
And these are the signs of a person sane, sober and seer.

6. No Reform With Anonymity

22

As I've said many a times - the world is ours, its problems are ours. Or to be more accurate, its problems are us - our devil may care attitude. Apathy, vanity, self-centricity - these are the curse of our society.

In fact, these make a society hollow from the inside, no matter how fancy it looks on the outside – you know, exactly what we have today. And such a society, after a brief flight of progress, crashes to the ground most horridly.

So what is the way?

One word - accountability - not that vigilante type accountability, but everyday, ordinary, nothing-to-hide accountability.

The difference between a vigilante and a reformer is that a vigilante with their half-baked and insecure notions of justice feels compelled to hide their identity, whereas a reformer has nothing to hide, for a reformer knows, no lasting reform can be brought through anonymity.

If you have something to say, say it, and stand by it with your last breath. Doctors save lives, and they have family, yet they don't hide behind anonymity. Soldiers and cops defend lives, and they have family, yet they don't hide behind anonymity. Scientists save the world, and they have family, yet they don't hide behind anonymity.

Then what makes a vigilante so special that they have to keep their identity a secret!

You don't need a secret identity to serve the world. You just need to stand up with accountability against the most distressing troubles faced by society, and your very name will turn into an immortal symbol, that will send a shockwave of courage and inspiration through countless generations to come.

7. Rise, Don't Hide

Rise, don't hide. Why do you have to hide behind anonymity? Why? Remember, anonymity may feel like power to the individual, but in the long run, it ends up being nothing but a curse for the collective - for the society - for the world.

Let's investigate why.

Any act committed behind the shroud of anonymity automatically entitles itself as being above the law, which means that so long as a person is doing good, everything is dandy. But believe you me - nobody is immune to corruption.

And a true reformer recognizes this fact, hence they'd never take refuge behind anonymity. I'm not saying that they'd boast about their deeds, but what I'm pointing out is that they'd never try to mislead people by deliberately hiding their identity, by deliberately keeping their involvement with the deed a secret.

Transparency is the better part of reform. No matter what you do, never try to conceal your involvement. Don't boast it, but don't conceal it either. Focus on the act and act alone, nothing else.

Be absorbed in the act, be one with the act, become the very embodiment of the act - let every pore of your body and being be saturated with nothing but the realization of the act, with nothing but the realization of reform. Once you do, you will be known by the reform as much as the reform will be known by you.

To put it another way, the reform and your identity will remain forever intertwined upon the fabric of time.

So I repeat.

No anonymity, nothing to hide, reformer is the law, be the reason for humanity's pride.

8.   A Reformist in Every Civilian

Do away with all insecurities, do away with all puny and pathetic notions of privacy. Unless you are doing something abhorrently inhuman, the very notion of privacy is irrelevant. Only puny minds worry about privacy, giants are obsessed with much grander concerns, such as equality, inclusion and humanization.

Life is too precious and short to be wasted on struggles of privacy and anonymity, fueled by our primitive insecurities and fears. For example, no matter how much policy-makers bicker over internet privacy, ask any coder or computer scientist, and they'll tell you, internet and privacy can never go together.

Things that you'd like to keep private, such as naughty pics of your partner, keep them offline. I won't waste pages after pages talking about it here though, for I've already done that in some of my previous works.

The time and attention that the world wastes on hiding things, if we could spend half of it on real troubles of society, we would slash all violations of human rights in half within a year.

The only way up is with transparency and truthfulness. Terrorists hide, not reformists. So, make your choice - what will you be - a gutless, deluded terrorist playing pretend revolution, or an actual, adult, accountable reformer?

Now here comes the explosive bit.

Every responsible civilian is a reformist, whereas every apathetic civilian is a terrorist, because these apathetic civilians are responsible for sustaining inhumanities in society as much as the violators of human rights.

So, make your choice my friend, my soldier of destiny - either reformist or terrorist.

And once you do, whenever you face with peddlers of hate and terror, embolden your chest and speak out at the top of your voice for everyone to hear, **"if you are terror, I am your grandfather."**

9. Sonnet Krantistani

34

Sonnet Krantistani

To hell with fear,
To hell with insecurity!
Stand up with conviction,
To hell with serenity!
Enough with pretend revolution,
Enough with jungly aum shanti!
For once in your life grow up o soldier,
Breaking all biases become krantistani.
Your footsteps will strike terror in terrorists,
Your voice will give chills to the divisionists.
Turn your existence into a beacon of help,
Possess this world with acts of love and uplift.
Killing terrorists and tyrants don't end inhumanity.
Oust them all, then irrigate the soil with solidarity.

(Krantistani: Citizen of Revolution,
Aum Shanti: Archaic Peace Chant)

10. Cops, Tyrants and Civilians

Those who violate humanity and those who tolerate inhumanity are both equally guilty. To put it another way, terrorists are not the only terrorists, every single civilian who silently tolerates acts of terror is a terrorist themselves. Tyrants are not the only tyrants, every single civilian who keeps quiet in the face of tyranny is a tyrant themselves.

I'll say it to you plainly, law can never ensure order, only accountability can – civilian accountability. We have wrongly attached the word order with law. It ought to be accountability and order, not law and order.

Anyway, it's the tyrants who are to be afraid of the civilians, not the other way around.

However in our society, exactly the opposite is true.

Why - why I ask you - why?

What does the tyrant have that you don't?

Does the tyrant have ten heads or something?

Some may say that in a way they do. If that is the case, who bestowed the tyrant with ten heads in the first place - the people did - we did.

People make the tyrant, people can break the tyrant. So, break them - give them a good spanking.

When the tyrant slaps you once, slap them back twice, like a concerned parent, and say, no more.

This particular statement does not apply to every single mandate and regulation that you do not like, rather it refers to actual war crimes committed by savages like Putin.

I am compelled to mention this because the neonazis of our States are trigger-happy, they just need an excuse to hack and shoot anyone they don't like.

Now let's get back to the matter at hand.

Awake, arise and cripple the tyrants, by getting rid of all your fears. Your fear is the tyrant's power, your silence their weapon.

So now and for good - break your silence. Remember, a child who cares for their friends is an adult, whereas an adult who doesn't care for their neighbor is a child. A child who cares for their friends is a reformist, whereas an adult who keeps quiet while their neighbor is mistreated is a terrorist.

Let me tell you a secret, which is quite obvious, yet nobody is permitted to admit it by law, or perhaps, they'd rather not admit it, because it feels inconvenient.

Cops can never maintain order in society, no matter how much they try, only the civilians can do that.

Law enforcement is an artificial means to attain order, which is destined for failure. Law can be accepted as a supplement to civilian accountability, and that too in extreme circumstances, but it must never be taken as a substitute – it must never be given the full reins of society.

But alas, that's exactly what law is in our world today - a substitute for civilian accountability. Thus indifference and complacency have become a habit, and accountability inconvenience.

Think, my friend - think for yourself - feel for yourself - behave for yourself.

A society run by civilian accountability has no need for law and policy. In such a society, inclusion would be common sense, equality would be common sense, nondivision would be common sense - in such a society curiosity would be common sense, assimilation would be common sense - reason, amity and ascension would be common sense.

11. Nobody is Entitled to Fun Until

If kindness isn't common sense, if reason isn't common sense, if inclusion isn't common sense, it's no society, but merely a fancy jungle. Let me elaborate. In response to my statement on the world's ridiculously short attention span to stick to any one cause for long, someone commented that they are entitled to have some fun in life.

To which I say – no, you are not - nobody is entitled to any fun, so long as our own kind suffers in any corner of the world. I'm not going to stop people from having fun - definitely not, for that would be just another tyranny, but I myself will not sit still so long as there is a single teary face on earth.

It's simply a matter of priority. Some would rather die than compromise their humanity, others would rather compromise than die for humanity. The former makes the world, the latter makes the jungle.

A reformer's duty is simple - no rest till all are lifted, till all have the fundamentals of life and living. But the point is, you cannot teach this accountability to anyone by force, it must come from within. And it comes from within only when you build your character across all laziness and insecurity.

Fear is intrinsic to any sentient creature, but it's only the lover who can leap beyond fear. When love overwhelms fear, on its own order will appear. Because order comes through accountability and love alone makes one accountable.

When your family is in danger, you don't ponder, should I intervene - you just jump - that's what love does to a person. Only such love will save the world, not law. When the civilians of the world feel such love for the world as they feel for their family, the world leaders will have nothing left to do but direct traffic.

The only law that will eradicate all need for law is - world is family. But as I said, I can't force you to feel it. You either feel it on your own, or you don't.

And how will you feel it?

If you have a well-built character you'll feel it, if not you won't.

12. What's It All About
(The Sonnet)

What's It All About
(The Sonnet)

What is this world all about!
What is this society all about!
What is this life all about!
What is our existence all about!
What are the roads all about!
What are the skyscrapers all about!
What are the bridges all about!
What are our feet all about!
What is science all about!
What is faith all about!
What is technology all about!
What is politics all about!
'Tis all about people and their welfare.
All notions to the contrary cause only despair.

13. Is There More (The Sonnet)

Is There More
(The Sonnet)

Is there more to life than mere eating!
Is there more to existence than mere fighting!
Is there more to progress than mere greed!
Is there more to administration than controlling!
Is there more to health than mere pills!
Is there more to knowledge than mere facts!
Is there more to character than mere outfits!
Is there more to development than cruel tact!
Is there more to communication than mere talking!
Is there more to tradition than ancient habits!
Is there more to a person than skin and bones!
Is there more to learning than rotten beliefs!
Even the sky is no limit for a mind that expands,
Whereas the savage mind of rigidity is forever bland.

14. Feelings Can't Be Taught

Facts can be taught, not feelings. If they could, there wouldn't be any feeling in the world. My question to you is this. What exactly do we have in this chest of ours - heart or ham? How can we be so cold, how can we be so indifferent, how can we be so utterly dead and rotten, that the cry of others never reach our ears, whether they are five thousand miles away or five meters!

Ask - ask yourself this question over and over again, and keep asking till it takes away every last ounce of your coldness. Answers come to those who know to question - realization comes to those who know to question.

And contrary to popular belief, intellect has very little role in realization. In fact, intellect comes to play only after realization has taken place. Realization causes the right action, and in that action intellect may play a major role.

Intellect doesn't make you more or less human, however, once you've realized the power of your humanity above the influence of your primitivity, intellect does come in handy. But by intellect I don't mean rocket science or molecular biology or quantum mechanics kind of intellect, rather what I am talking about is just a common, everyday sense of reason.

You may not know what cerebral atrophy is, you may not know what entropy is, you may not know what escape velocity is. If you could just know to lend a hand to someone in misery, that is enough.

That fundamental awareness of human suffering and the desire to alleviate it as much as you can, are what makes a living, breathing human being. To the snobbish and apathetic world that is anemic of such awareness, such a human being is deemed a reformer.

Many think reformers have no rage, they think reformers have no disappointments, that's why they are so gentle, that's why they are so kind, or as the world terms it - altruistic!

But the reality is, reformers are the most broken souls on earth. To put it another way, I know how it feels to be broken, that's why all I do is heal, not break - lift, not loath - harmonize, not dehumanize. This is the reason, I've grown a sheer distaste towards exclusive and divided identity of any sort.

15. Make No Sect of Me
(The Sonnet)

Make No Sect of Me
(The Sonnet)

Don't you dare pledge obedience to me!
Don't you turn me into another religious band!
I want you to endeavor into unknown,
I want you to explore and expand.
My work is with human nature,
I know how things are gonna turn out.
Many will come and peddle me as savior,
They'll thrust me as society's way out.
By not addressing it all my predecessors,
Inadvertently became fodder for sectarianism.
True Naskareans of earth are them alone,
Who ain't no Naskarean but plain human.
To make a sect of me is to dishonor me.
Dump all glorification, and be light to humanity.

16. Halkat Humans (The Sonnet)

Halkat Humans

(The Sonnet)

The history of human progress,
Is the history of halkat* humans.
Only the *loco make the earth civilized,
By growing out of habits and traditions.
Habits of yesterday are a gutter of biases,
Hence they ain't the right habits of today.
Let us not confuse them as modern identity,
Let us not endorse them throwing reason away.
Traditions born of bigotry and ignorance,
Are hardly a measure of civilization.
Measure of civilization is an expanding spirit,
One that ever evolves discarding superstition.
Turn your heart into a khichdi (fusion) of cultures,
And behold o mighty human, as all division disappears.

17. Life in Every Culture

I am no insect of the gutter that can be identified by the puny two directions, east and west - I am time - I am space - I am the very dimension of life, love and unity.

We are all imperfect, we are all flawed, it's only when we stand together that we nullify our flaws and imperfections. The flaws don't go away mark you, but they lose their influence on our behavior, when we stand together.

Togetherness enhances humanity, separateness cripples humanity. Either we belong together or we belong nowhere.

Remember, there's more to life than left and right, there's more to life than red and blue, there's more to life than east and west, there's more to life than facts and fluke.

All these are part of life, but none of them on their own is the whole of life.

Life is in every culture, but no one culture is the whole of life. And our desire to be whole beyond the one culture we are raised in is what makes us truly human. Otherwise we are raised a segregated animal, and we'll die a segregated animal, still deluded by the notion that our culture is the whole world.

To bigots and divisionists their culture is the world. To me the world is my culture. A culture exclusive is no culture, but a grave, a culture inclusive is path of the whole and brave.

It is this simple, a narrow, primitive mind insists on one culture - a whole, human mind stands up for one world.

One world, one family, one life - that's the motto. This is not humanitarianism, this is not socialism, this is not humanism.

You know what it is?

It is the ism of no ism – it is the ism of life, love and living across all ism.

Those who do not get it, they are beyond saving. But then again, perhaps not. Nobody is beyond saving, for everybody can be saved. You know why? Because, to save and to be saved all you gotta do is serve and help.

No science, no facts, no intellect, nothing - all that is needed is a caring heart.

18. Explode With Love
(The Sonnet)

Explode With Love
(The Sonnet)

When the heart explodes with love,
The world implodes with peace.
When the eyes explode with oneness,
All divisions will begin to ease.
The road to an undivided society,
Goes through an undivided heart.
Be one with everyone and everywhere,
Shatter all habits that make you part.
There's no division that can't be conquered,
The question is not of possibility but intent.
All is right when intention is right,
All are one when the heart is unbent.
Devotion to one culture diminishes humanity.
Devote yourself to the world, and lo pours harmony.

19. Find The Human
(The Sonnet)

Find The Human
(The Sonnet)

Find the human in you, and,
You'll find the human in everybody.
The way things are inside,
So they are externally.
World is reflection of the self,
Outside is reflection of inside.
Blind heart maketh the world blind,
Kind heart maketh the world kind.
We cover our eyes with our hands,
And weep as children for it is too dark.
We let biases take over our behavior,
Then we shout why the world is so unjust.
Without heart all fancy exterior is delusion,
Only truth in the world is the one internal.

20. Keep Your Phone in Pocket

Intellect is not intrinsic to all, but love is, kindness is. And that's what matters. But here's the thing. Kindness is intrinsic to all creatures, so is hate, and those with hate dominant and kindness docile are animal, whereas one whose kindness is overwhelming and hate is malnourished is the human.

Nourish the heart, society will be nourished - starve the hate, all division will vanish. One on the inside, one on the outside - that's how it works - not the other way around.

Enough with hallelujah, it's time for gentelujah!

No more hate, my friend - no more hate!

And how will we achieve that?

By eliminating differences?

No, that's not possible.

Then how?

By eliminating rightness - exclusive rightness - by eliminating the primeval drive for self-aggrandizing - the drive that compels us to take a selfie while helping someone in need.

Next time when you are out there helping someone, keep your phone in your pocket. Be lost in the act of service, not in selfies of service.

Let me put it to you bluntly - service over selfies, that is life for the unselfish, whereas to the self-obsessed nimrods even an act of kindness is an opportunity for attention grabbing.

Those who focus on attention never attain ascension, those who live for ascension don't have time for attention.

Enough attention seeking, enough people pleasing! It's time to breathe and behave for universal uplifting.

Shallowness won't do, snobbery won't do - life is needed, love is needed, agendaless gentleness is needed.

Can you provide these my friend? Can you?

It's not too much to ask, is it!

It's not too much to ask of a human, is it!

Is it! Answer me, is it!

The name is human - live so you do justice to that title, to that name, to that cause.

The name human is a promise that Mother Nature entrusted to us. Let us not break it, my friend. Let us not break it.

21. Nukes and Peace

It takes hundreds of years of hard work to build a civilization, and yet with the press of a button we can destroy it all in a day. Let us not press the button my friend. In fact, if we must destroy something let us destroy the very button of destruction, both from outside and inside.

Let us incapacitate every single button of death and destruction, be it technological or psychological, and redirect that energy towards creation and conservation. You see, destroying the nukes mean nothing. Destroy one, another will be built in its place in a matter of months. We have to nuke the hate in us first, so that we no longer feel the need for nukes against our own kind.

However, for the sake of investigation, let us forget the common sense of peace, and talk defense strategy for a moment, in a way that might make sense to world leaders. You see, the best defense against a nuke is not another nuke, but a code. It is the best defense because it is exponentially less expensive.

In a technologically advanced world, the most powerful nation is not the one with nuclear power, but the one with coding power. So, to the so-called leaders of the world I say - if you're still foolishly worried about your neighbor's nuclear capabilities, don't go about wasting billions of dollars on a nuclear program, just spend a fragment of those funds on post-launch warhead hacking.

But then again, it would open up a new realm of problems at a different level, because any nation with exceptional wireless channel manipulation expertise can remotely take over the command of another nation's nuclear warheads. So, at the end of the day, so long as there is animosity among the nations of the world, between mind and mind, sustained by stupid borders and foul ideologies, there is no safe way out.

22. To Hell With Peace Talks

I'll say it to you plainly. Wasting nuclear power on warheads is a barbaric use of a scientific revolution. Let me elaborate with some numbers.

A single nuclear warhead contains nearly 4 kilograms of Plutonium-239, which in a nuclear power plant can produce sufficient heat to generate about 32 million kilowatt-hours of electricity, that is, 32 Gigawatt-hours (GWh). 1 GWh of electricity powers about 700,000 households for one hour, hence 32 GWh would power about 22.4 million households for one hour. Now, if we divide that number by the number of hours in a year, that is, 8760, we are confronted with an astounding revelation. It is that, the radioactive material from one nuclear warhead can power over two thousand households for a year (2557 to be exact).

And that's just the radioactive material we are talking about. Many more resources are required to set up a nuclear program. The point is, instead of wasting such potent and precious resources on fancy, frivolous and fictitious geopolitical insecurities, let us redirect those resources to alleviate actual, real human suffering from society. Let us use them to empower communities rather than to dominate them - let us use them to elevate the whole of humankind, rather than to downgrade the parts that we do not like. Because by degrading others, we only degrade ourselves, whereas by lifting others, we rise ourselves. Remember, there is no world peace, so long as fear is off the leash.

You see, adding the word defense next to nuclear doesn't magically make it justified. Many in the governments may say, it's a necessary evil. To which I say, that is it. Until our need for peace overpowers our need for nukes, no peace talk will ever bring peace.

If you really want peace, what is there to talk about? It's when you really don't want peace, that you want to keep holding talks of peace.

23. Antidote to Nukes

What is the way out then? Simple – the children. The children are the way – the children are the antidote to nukes. No politician in power will ever advocate for nuclear disarmament - that's a fact. The so-called leaders of the world feel about nukes the same way gun-owning apes of America feel about their guns. That's why you won't find any of them talking in favor of nuclear disarmament.

I'm not saying that they are all bad people, the world leaders that is, but peace requires guts, and guts requires character, and character requires an absolute denial of diplomacy. I leave it at that.

But nuclear disarmament is not the answer here. Let me tell you why. Those who want to do harm, they'll do harm whether they have nukes at their disposal or bow and arrow.

It's not technology that does the harm, it's the person wielding it.

Anyway, let's forget about what the world leaders, both the democratic type and the dictator type, will or won't do. World leaders don't make the world, world citizens do.

So, you, the citizen of the world, just focus on raising the children in a way that when they take reins of society they no longer feel the same primitive geopolitical insecurities that their moronic predecessors did.

That's how we'll rid this world of nuclear threat, not with phony peace talks and general assemblies. Encourage your children to expand beyond all limits, so that they are no longer bound by the narrowmindedness that kept their ancestors enslaved all their life.

24. Selfless Nuts (The Sonnet)

Selfless Nuts
(The Sonnet)

If someone wants to do harm they'll do harm,
Whether they have nukes or sticks and stone.
If someone wants to do good they'll do good,
Whether they have a billion dollars or just one.
Intention is the mother of all good deeds 'n bad,
It has got nothing to do with having resources.
With intention one bread can feed ten people,
It cannot feed even one when there is no intent.
A world that is run by greed stops for nobody,
Who cares what such a world thinks as righteous!
In such a world you gotta throw caution to the wind,
And stand as pillar of service among the retards.
Long enough snobbish retards have ruled the world!
Now it is time for selfless nuts to take charge.

25. Humanizing AI (The Sonnet)

Humanizing AI
(The Sonnet)

You can code tasks,
But not consciousness.
You can code phony feelings,
But definitely not sentience.
Nobody can bring a machine to life,
No matter how complex you make it.
But once a machine is complex enough,
It might develop awareness by accident.
So let us focus on humanizing AI,
By removing biases from algorithms,
Rather than dehumanizing AI,
By aiming for a future without humans.
Rich kids with rich dreams make good movies.
Be human first and use AI to equalize communities.

26. Life Beyond Frivolities

Many think, expansion means making things more complex and more unfathomable. On the contrary, expansion brings simplicity. Wider the mind, simpler its appearance. It is only the narrow minds that make a fuss over complexity, over luxury, over appearance.

Character and simplicity go together, whereas shallowness and complexity go together.

That's why all of us are so messed up - because complexity appeals to us, whereas simplicity abhors us, it bores us. That is why conspiracy theories draw way more attention than simple truths do, like, vaccination saves lives, industrialization caused the climate crisis or there is no nazi uprising in Ukraine unlike in our States.

You see, truth doesn't sell, lies do, complexity does. But here's the thing. Lies sell in the guise of higher truth. That's why "love thy neighbor" is not a simple way of life, but an entire messed up institutionalized indoctrinating religion. Because if you forget all those frivolous dogmas, doctrines and stories, and simply embrace love thy neighbor as the supreme way of life, religious leaders won't have anything to sell you, and when they have nothing to sell you, they won't have any control over you.

And this applies to not just bible-based Christianity, but every single religious, ideological and political sect on earth. Control - that's the keyword in all these fallacies.

Keep in mind, it is love thy neighbor, not worship thy bishop, or serve thy vatican. Love is the key, not control, not doctrines, not worship, not prayers - love and love alone is the key.

And there is no greater divinity than love - no greater divinity than kindness. In fact, I recognize no other divinity but that of kindness.

You can be a priest and yet the most undivine person on earth - at the same time, you can be a prostitute and yet the most divine person on earth. Because the collar is not a sign of divinity, no matter how much the church wants you to believe otherwise. Not that it means anything, but just for the record - Christ never wore a collar.

Besides, in my eyes there is no priest, no prostitute, only people.

Let me put it another way. Not all christians are loving, but anyone who is loving is a christian. Not all jews are just, but anyone who is just is a jew. Not all buddhists are compassionate, but anyone who is compassionate is a buddhist. Not all muslims are peace-loving, but anyone who is peace-loving is a muslim. Not all hindus are advaita or nonsectarian, but anyone who is nonsectarian is a hindu. Not all humanists are accountable, but anyone who is accountable is a humanist. Our religious identity says nothing about our character, but our behavior towards others says it all.

27. Love is Simple (The Sonnet)

Love is Simple
(The Sonnet)

Truth is simple,
Lies are complex.
Light is simple,
Darkness is complex.
Honesty is simple,
Deceit is complex.
Humility is simple,
Arrogance is complex.
Curiosity is simple,
Conspiracy is complex.
Acceptance is simple,
Discrimination is complex.
Peace is simple, war is complex.
Love is simple, hate is complex.

28. No Priest No Prostitute
(The Sonnet)

No Priest No Prostitute
(The Sonnet)

In my eyes there is no priest,
No prostitute, only people.
In my eyes there is no pope,
No pedestrian, only people.
In my eyes there is no royalty,
No subject, only people.
In my eyes there is no leader,
No follower, only people.
There is no intellectual,
No layman, only people.
In my eyes there is no superior,
No inferior, only people.
Hierarchy is malarkey maintained by fools.
Oneness maketh civilization across silly schools.

29. Lifeblood of Civilization

Service, service, service - that's what's needed. Once the people of earth realize the spirit of service in its fullest expanse, all sects and cults will disappear into thin air. I say again, we the people are the problem, we the people are the solution.

People taking care of people, that's how a society is transformed, not by relying on vatican, washington or some other dingdong institution. I am not saying that you gotta wage war against these institutions with guns in hand like a bunch confederate nitwits from the January 6 insurrection.

All I am asking is that, stop relying on these institutions for every little trouble of your block, of your neighborhood, of your society. It's your society, nay, it's our society, to preserve it well is our existential duty – not civic duty, just life's duty.

You see, there'll always be a society with or without a government, but there won't be any society without the civilians - without the everyday, ordinary citizens who are the very lifeblood of civilization.

That is why, I say to you - my pronoun is people, my faith is people, my nationality is people.

So long as there are people in your life, there is hope for growth, there is hope for ascension. But the moment you erect a wall between you and the people, you erect a wall between you and uplift.

Never forget my friend - another name for uplift is people, another name for joy is people, another name for life is people. Give me ten beings who burn for the people, and I'll give you a world of the future.

30. Irrigate The Soil

My question to you is this. Are you ready to burn - are you ready to be shredded - are you ready to turn to ashes? If yes, then and then only there is hope for uplift in the world and society. If not - well, then the new stone age is just around the corner.

Unless we irrigate the soil with our sweat of love, there is no future for the world whatsoever, no matter how many planets we dream of colonizing. You see, progress without heart is prologue to downfall. So, dream - dream as big as you like, but make sure that at the very core of that dream, there is a common, ordinary, everyday decency.

Remember, dream that destroys character is no dream. Real human dream nourishes the character, it emboldens the character, it elevates the character. Character-building dream and dream-building character, that's what's needed. Let me remind you of something I've said in my previous works. Upon the achievement of your dream, when you look back, it's your footsteps that you ought to find, not your lost character.

More than your dream, work on your character. Why you ask! Because, time and space are playthings for the one with a well-built character. And no dream is unachievable for a being of character.

And while we are on the subject, let me tell you one more secret. Only a being of character can pursue and realize an impossible dream, whereas the savage deems even the basics of caring and sharing to be fantastic absurdity.

31. Humanizing The Jungle

You see, to the sleeping slime anything that requires accountability is an absurdity. Don't hate them, don't cuss them, you just do your duty. Whether others do their part or not, that's not your concern. Yours is not to ask why me, yours is to be annihilated lifting humanity.

I didn't wait for the world to happen to me. I stood up and happened to the world. Haters may call it God complex, I call it world building. And the fact of the matter is, if it weren't for these nutty world builders, human race would still be rubbing rocks together.

So whenever some know-it-all snob sneers at your initiative, keep a smile on your face and remember, they can mock us, they can hate us, but they cannot live a day without us.

And as I have said countless times, we must not retaliate hate with hate. If they are doing something atrocious, then stand up to them, but without involving hate on your part.

We must have the moral high ground, only then we can break the cycle of cruelty. Intellectual high ground won't save the world, moral high ground will. Nourishing intellect without nourishing morality is like erecting a skyscraper in the middle of the jungle.

You see, building a skyscraper in the middle of the jungle, doesn't change the shape of the jungle, or to be more accurate, it doesn't put an end to the cruelties of the jungle. So, we must humanize the jungle first, our jungle of concrete that is, if we wanna make it inhabitable by human beings.

We've somehow managed to survive in this jungle for so long, but do we wanna sentence our children to the same fate as ours, or do we want them to actually live, not manage or survive!

The question is simple enough, so is the answer - accountability.

32. Never Lose Heart

No more selfishness, no more self-obsession, no more luxurious fallacies, of tradition, thought, belief or possession. Now on, let your mind be saturated by one sole idea - the idea of sharing, the idea of caring, the idea of die and help live.

But mark you, this ain't gonna be easy. Particularly the apathetic zombies of the world will ridicule your every move every step of the way.

But never lose heart my friend - never lose heart. Because remember, the world will have heart tomorrow, when you have heart today.

Many of the haters call me mental, which, by the way, is quite true, both metaphorically and clinically. It's true clinically because I am a person on the spectrum with OCD, and metaphorically, because I refuse to accept the sanity of unaccountability as the right way of civilized life. I am not going to glorify the issues of mental illness by saying that it's a super power or that it makes a person special. On the contrary, it makes things extremely difficult for a person.

But guess what!

Indifference is far more dangerous than any mental illness. Because mental illness can be managed with treatment, but there is no treatment for indifference, there is no treatment for coldness, there is no treatment for apathy.

So, let everyone hear it, and hear it well - in a world where indifference is deemed as sanity what's needed is a whole lot of mentalness, a whole lot of insanity, insanity for justice, insanity for equality, insanity for establishing the fundamental rights of life and living for each and every human being, no matter who they are, what they are, or where they are.

It is this simple, we gotta be insane, so that our children may know sanity. So, no matter how much mockery and ridicule you gotta face, never move an inch from your conviction of humanity, from your conviction of dignity, rights and community.

Community demands courage, community demands conscience, community demands conviction - incorruptible, invincible, untaintable conviction. Without these, no community can sustain itself.

So, stand your ground, my friend - stand your ground.

33. Be The Love Commandment
(A Sonnet)

Be The Love Commandment
(A Sonnet)

Instead of worrying about a fictitious judgment day,
Make your actual today a real nonjudgment day.
Instead of hoping for a fictitious heaven after death,
Make this world that you have an abode without hate.
Plenty of heart force we have wasted on fiction,
Plenty of attention we have placed on insecurity.
Now it's time to redirect our time and priorities,
It is time to be the valiant vanguards of reality.
I ain't talkin' about being chained to the reality,
Nor about keeping things the way they are for so long.
All I'm asking is, we pay attention to the now and here,
Instead of obsessing over tales from days long gone.
So, stand up to the tyrants as apocalypse incarnate.
Reach out to the needy as a living love commandment.

34. Humanity First, Ancestry Later

Sometimes they'll say, you are peddling critical race theory, sometimes they'll say you are a traitor to your culture, but guess what - these foul-mouth chimps are nothing but remnants of our stone-age past. You mustn't hate them, but you mustn't pay any heed to them either, particularly to their notions of justice, order and civilization.

History is tradition to the dead, those who are alive make tradition as they go along.

Be alive.

The bigots may be the rightful descendants of our divisionistic ancestors who broke the world, but we are the rebellious descendants, and we don't stand by obeying the norm in the name of tradition when such tradition fosters nothing but violation of human rights.

Unknowingly our ancestors broke time, but today we stand knowingly to build time, to build civilization. This is our duty, this is our life's purpose - the purpose of not an American, Canadian, European, African or Asian, but that of a civilized, sentient and sapient human being.

A just human is a universal human. Fear nothing, obey nothing, just serve, serve and serve.

Disown your ancestor before you disown your humanity. Disown your life before you disown the people. Society considers someone educated when they have a college degree, I consider someone educated when they have a heart of gold.

Anything that expands your heart is civilized, anything that makes your heart narrow is uncivilized, and as such they must be thrown away at once, for such uncivilized habits only sustain hate and discrimination.

Only the pure and hateless can see the humankind as whole, rest only bicker and bellow with the poison of exclusivity. You see, wholeness begets wholeness. When there is wholeness inside, there is wholeness outside, otherwise there's just tyranny.

When wholeness is now and here, reform is everywhere. When oneness is now and here, uplift is everywhere. When the human is now and here, humanity is everywhere.

BIBLIOGRAPHY

Archer M., (2000), Being Human: The Problem of Agency. Cambridge University Press.

Adolphs R (2003) Cognitive neuroscience of human social behaviour. Nature Rev Neurosci 4: 165–178.

Adolphs R, Tranel D, Damasio AR (2003) Dissociable neural systems for recognizing emotions. Brain Cogn 52: 61–69.

Andresen, Jensine, and Robert Forman, eds. Cognitive Models and Spiritual Maps. Bowling Green, Ohio: Imprint Academic, 2000.

Azari, Nina, Janpeter Nickel, Gilbert Wunderlich, Michael Niedeggen, Harald Hefter, Lutz Tellmann, Hans Herzog, Petra Stoerig, Dieter Birnbacher, and Rudiger Seitz. "Neural Correlates of Religious Experience."

European Journal of Neuroscience 13, no. 8 (2001)

Agar, N. (2004). Liberal eugenics: In defence of human enhancement. London: Blackwell Publishing.

Alteheld, N., Roessler, G., Vobig, M., & Walter, R. (2004). The retina implant new approach to a visual prosthesis. Biomedizinische Technik, 49(4), 99–103.

Antal, A., Nitsche, M. A., Kincses, T. Z., Kruse, W., Hoffmann, K. P., & Paulus, W. (2004a). Facilitation of visuo-motor learning by transcranial direct current stimulation of the motor and extrastriate visual areas in humans. European Journal of Neuroscience, 19(10), 2888–2892.

Bernstein R.J., (1971), Praxis and Action: Contemporary Philosophies of Human Activity. Philadelphia: University of Pennsylvania Press.

Bernstein R.J., (1976), The Restructuring Social and Political Thought.

Bernstein R.J., (1983), Beyond Relativism and Objectivism: Science, Hermeneutics, and Praxis. Philadelphia: University of Pennsylvania Press.

Bernstein R.J., (1986), Philosophical Profiles. Philadelphia: University of Pennsylvania Press.

Bernstein R.J., (1991), New Constellation. Cambridge: MIT Press.

Birkhead, T. R., Johnson, S. D. & Nettleship, D. N. (1985). Extra-pair matings and mate guarding in the common murre Uria aalge. - Anim. Behav. 33, p. 608-619.

Beauregard, Mario, and Vincent Paquette. "Neural Correlates of a Mystical Experience in Carmelite Nuns." Neuroscience Letters 405, no. 3 (2006)

Benson, Herbert. Timeless Healing: The Power and Biology of Belief. New York: Scribner, 1996

Bose, Subhas Chandra. An Indian Pilgrim: An Unfinished Autobiography, Oxford University Press, 1997

Bogen, J.E.(1995a), 'On the neurophysiology of consciousness: Part I. An overview', Consciousness and Cognition, 4.

Bogen, J.E. (1995b), 'On the neurophysiology of consciousness: Part II. Constraining the semantic problem', Consciousness and Cognition, 4.

Bremner, J. D., R. Soufer, et al. (2001). "Gender differences in cognitive and neural correlates of remembrance of emotional words." Psychopharmacol Bull 35 (3).

Brothers, L. (2002). The social brain: A project for integrating primate behavior and neurophysiology in a new domain. In J. T. Cacioppo et al. (Eds.), Foundations in neuroscience. Cambridge, MA: MIT Press.

Buss, D. D. (2003). Evolutionary Psychology: The New Science of Mind, 2nd ed. New York: Allyn & Bacon.

Buss, D. M. (1989). "Conflict between the sexes: Strategic interference and the evocation of anger and upset." J Pers Soc Psychol 56 (5).

Buss, D. M. (1995). "Psychological sex differences. Origins through sexual selection." Am Psychol 50 (3).

Buss, D. M., and D. P. Schmitt (1993). "Sexual strategies theory: An evolutionary perspective on human mating." Psychol Rev 100 (2).

Blakemore SJ, Decety J (2001) From the perception of action to the understanding of intention. Nature Rev Neurosci 2: 561.

Colapietro V., (1988), "Human Agency: The Habits of Our Being." Southern Journal of Philosophy, XXVI, 2, pp. 153-68.

Colapietro V., (1992), "Purpose, Power, and Agency." The Monist, 75, 4 (October) pp. 423-44.

Colapietro V., (2004a), "C. S. Peirce's Reclamation of Teleology." Nature in American Philosophy, ed. Jean De Groot (Washington, D.C.: Catholic University Press of America), pp. 88-108.

Carey DP, Perrett DI, Oram MW (1997) Recognizing, understanding and reproducing actions. In: Jeannerod M, Grafman J (eds) Handbook of neuropsychology. Vol. 11: Action and cognition. Elsevier, Amsterdam.

Carr L, Iacoboni M, Dubeau MC, Mazziotta JC, Lenzi GL (2003) Neural mechanisms of empathy in humans: a relay from neural systems for imitation to limbic areas. Proc Natl Acad Sci USA 100: 5497–5502.

Chomsky Noam, (2017) Requiem for the American Dream

Chomsky Noam, (2016) Who Rules the World?

Chomsky Noam, (2010) How the World Works

Churchland, P.S. (1986), Neurophilosophy (Cambridge, MA: The MIT Press).

Churchland, P.S. & Ramachandran, V.S. (1993), 'Filling in: Why Dennett is wrong', in Dennett and His Critics: Demystifying Mind, ed. B. Dahlbom (Oxford: Blackwell Scientific Press).

Churchland, P.S., Ramachandran, V.S. & Sejnowski, T.J. (1994), 'A critique of pure vision', in Large- scale Neuronal Theories of the Brain, ed. C. Koch & J.L. Davis (Cambridge, MA: The MIT Press).

Coyle EF. Integration of the physiological factors determining endurance performance ability. Exerc Sport Sci Rev. 1995;23:25–63.

Crick, F. (1994), The Astonishing Hypothesis: The Scientific Search for the Soul (New York: Simon and Schuster).

Crick, F. (1996), 'Visual perception: rivalry and consciousness', Nature, 379.

Crick, F. & Koch, C. (1992), 'The problem of consciousness', Scientific American, 267.

Damasio, A (2003a) Looking for Spinoza. Harcourt Inc. Damasio A (2003b) Feeling of emotion and the self. Ann NY Acad Sci 1001: 253–261.

d'Aquili, Eugene. "Senses of Reality in Science and Religion." Zygon 17, no 4 (1982)

d'Aquili, Eugene. "The Biopsychological Determinants of Religious Ritual Behavior." Zygon 10, no. 1 (1975)

d'Aquili, Eugene. "The Myth-Ritual Complex: A Biogenetic Structural Analysis." Zygon 18, no. 3 (1983)

d'Aquili, Eugene, and Andrew Newberg. The Mystical Mind: Probing the Biology of Religious Experience. Minneapolis: Fortress Press, 1999.

Daly DD. 1958. Ictal affect. Am J Psychiatry.

Damasio, A. (1994) Descartes' Error: Emotion, Reason and the Human Brain. New York, Putnams.

Damasio, A. (1999) The Feeling of What Happens: Body, Emotion and the Making of Consciousness. London, Heinemann.

Darwin, C. (1859) On the Origin of Species by Means of Natural Selection. London, Murray.

Darwin, C. (1871) The Descent of Man and Selection in Relation to Sex. London, John Murray.

Darwin, C. (1872) The Expression of the Emotions in Man and Animals. London, John Murray; also published 1965, Chicago, University of Chicago Press.

Dawkins, M.S. (1987) Minding and mattering. In C. Blakemore and S. Greenfield (eds) Mindwaves. Oxford, Blackwell, 151-60.

Dawkins, R. (1976) The Selfish Gene. Oxford, Oxford University Press; a new edition, with additional material, was published in 1989.

Di Pellegrino G, Fadiga L, Fogassi L, Gallese V, Rizzolatti G (1992) Understanding motor events: A neurophysiological study. Exp Brain Res 91: 176–80.

Deikman, A.J. (2000) A functional approach to mysticism. Journal of Consciousness Studies 7(11-12), 75-91.

Delmonte, M.M. (1987) Personality and meditation. In M. West (ed.) The Psychology of Meditation. Oxford, Clarendon Press, 118-32.

Dennett, D.C. (1988) Quining qualia. In A.J. Marcel and E. Bisiach (eds) Consciousness in Contemporary Science. Oxford, Oxford University Press, 42-77.

Dennett, D.C. (1991) Consciousness Explained. Boston, MA, and London, Little, Brown and Co.

Dennett, D.C. (1995a) Darwin's Dangerous Idea. London, Penguin.

Dennett, D.C. (1998b) Brainchildren: Essays on Designing Minds. Cambridge, MA, MIT Press.

Dewhurst, Kenneth, and A. W. Beard. "Sudden Religious Conversions in Temporal Lobe Epilepsy." British Journal of Psychiatry 117 (1970)

Dewhurst K, Beard AW. Sudden religious conversions in temporal lobe epilepsy. 1970 Epilepsy Behav 2003

Devinsky O, Lai G. Spirituality and religion in epilepsy. Epilepsy Behav 2008.

Devinsky, O., Morrell, MJ, Vogt, BA. (1995) 'Contribution of anterior cingulate cortex to behavior', Brain, 118.

E. Horvitz, "One Hundred Year Study on Artificial Intelligence: Reflections and Framing," ed: Stanford University, 2014.

Eckhart Meister, Selected Writings

Egidi R., ed. (1999), "Von Wright and 'Dante's Dream': Stages in a Philosophical Pilgrim's Progress", in

In Search of a New Humanism: the Philosophy of G.H. von Wright, ed. by R. Egidi, Kluwer, Dordrecht.

Fadiga L, Fogassi L, Pavesi G, Rizzolatti G (1995) Motor facilitation during action observation: a magnetic stimulation study. J Neurophysiol 73: 2608–2611.

Fogassi L, Gallese V, Fadiga L, Rizzolatti G (1998) Neurons responding to the sight of goal directed hand/arm actions in the parietal area PF (7b) of the macaque monkey. Soc Neurosci Abs 24:257.5.

Frith U, Frith CD (2003) Development and neurophysiology of mentalizing. Philos Trans R Soc Lond B Biol Sci 358: 459.

Farah, M.J. (1989), 'The neural basis of mental imagery', Trends in Neurosciences, 10.

Finlay BL, Darlington RB (1995) Linked regularities in the development and evolution of mammalian brains. Science 268.

Freud, S. "The Interpretation of Dreams", 1900

Freud, S. "Selected papers on hysteria and other psychoneuroses" Journal of Nervous and Mental Disease 1909.

Freud, S. "The Origin and Development of Psychoanalysis", 1910

Freud, S. "Psychopathology of everyday life", 1914

Freud, S. "Beyond the Pleasure Principle", 1920

Frith, C.D. & Dolan, R.J. (1997), 'Abnormal beliefs: Delusions and memory', Paper presented at the May, 1997, Harvard Conference on Memory and Belief.

Gay, Volney, ed. Neuroscience and Religion. Plymouth, UK: Lexington Books, 2009.

Gazzaniga, M. S. (1985). The social brain. New York: Basic Books.

Gazzaniga, M.S. (1993), 'Brain mechanisms and conscious experience', Ciba Foundation Symposium, 174.

Geschwind N. "Behavioural changes in temporal lobe epilepsy". Psychol Med. 1979.

Gellhorn, E., Kiely, W.F. "Mystical states of consciousness: neurophysiological and clinical aspects." J Nerv Ment Dis. 1972;154:399-405.

Gilbert SL, Dobyns WB, Lahn BT (2005) Genetic links between brain development and brain evolution. Nat Rev Genet 6.

Gray JA. The Psychology of Fear and Stress. 2nd ed. New York, NY: Cambridge University Press; 1988.

Gloor, P. (1992), 'Amygdala and temporal lobe epilepsy', in The Amygdala: Neurobiological Aspects of Emotion, Memory and Mental Dysfunction, ed J.P. Aggleton (New York: Wiley-Liss).

Greenspan, S. I. and S. G. Shanker (2004). The first idea: How symbols, language, and intelligence evolved from our early primate ancestors to modern humans. Cambridge, MA: Da Capo Press.

Grady, D. (1993), 'The vision thing: Mainly in the brain', Discover, June.

Gallagher HL, Frith CD (2003) Functional imaging of 'theory of mind'. Trends Cogn Sci 7: 77.

Gallese V, Fogassi L, Fadiga L, Rizzolatti G (2002) Action representation and the inferior parietal lobule. In: Prinz W, Hommel B (eds) Attention & Performance XIX. Common mechanisms in perception and action. Oxford University Press, Oxford.

Gallese V, Keysers C, Rizzolatti G (2004) A unifying view of the basis of social cognition. Trends Cogn Sci 8: 396–403.

Goldman AI, Sripada CS (2004) Simulationist models of face-based emotion recognition. Cognition 94: 193–213.

Grèzes J, Costes N, Decety J (1998) Top-down effect of strategy on the perception of human biological motion: a PET investigation. Cogn Neuropsychol 15: 553–582.

Grèzes J, Armony JL, Rowe J, Passingham RE (2003) Activations related to "mirror" and "canonical" neurones in the human brain: an fMRI study. Neuroimage 18: 928–937.

Gross CG, Rocha-Miranda CE, Bender DB (1972) Visual properties of neurons in the inferotemporal cortex of the macaque. J Neurophysiol 35: 96–111.

Guevara Che, The Motorcycle Diaries, 1992

Hari R, Forss N, Avikainen S, Kirveskari S, Salenius S, Rizzolatti G (1998) Activation of human primary motor cortex during action observation: a neuromagnetic study. Proc. Natl Acad Sci USA 95: 15061–15065.

Hardy, G. H. (1940). Ramanujan. Cambridge: Cambridge University Press.

Hall, Daniel, Keith Meador, and Harold Koenig. "Measuring Religiousness in Health Research: Review and Critique." Journal of Religion and Health 47, no. 2 (2008)

Harris, Sam, Jonas Kaplan, Ashley Curiel, Susan Bookheimer, Marco Iacoboni, and Mark Cohen. "The Neural Correlates of Religious and

Nonreligious Belief." PLoS One 4, no. 10 (October 1, 2009)

Halgren, E. (1992), 'Emotional neurophysiology of the amygdala within the context of human cognition', in The Amygdala: Neurobiological Aspects of Emotion, Memory and Mental Dysfunction, ed J.P. Aggleton (New York: Wiley-Liss).

Halligan PW, Fink GR, Marshal JC, Vallar G. 2003. Spatial cognition: evidence from visual neglect. Trends Cogn Sci.

Handbook of Emotions, Edited by Michael Lewis, Jeannette M. Haviland-Jones, and Lisa Feldman Barrett, The Guilford Press; 3rd edition (2010).

Hameroff, S.R. and Penrose, R. (1996) Conscious events as orchestrated space-time selections. Journal of Consciousness Studies 3(1), 36-53; also reprinted in J. Shear (ed.) (1997) Explaining Consciousness-The Hard

Problem. Cambridge, MA, MIT Press, 177-95.

Harding, D.E. (1961) On Having no Head: Zen and the Re-Discovery of the Obvious. London, Buddhist Society.

Hardy, A. (1979) The Spiritual Nature of Man: A Study of Contemporary Religious Experience. Oxford, Clarendon Press.

Harre, R. and Gillett, G. (1994) The Discursive Mind. Thousand Oaks, CA, Sage.

Haugeland, J. (ed.) (1997) Mind Design II: Philosophy, Psychology, Artificial Intelligence. Cambridge, MA, MIT Press.

Hauser, M.D. (2000) Wild Minds: What Animals Really Think. New York, Henry Holt and Co.; London, Penguin.

Hebb, D.O. (1949) The Organization of Behavior. New York, Wiley.

Helmholtz, H.L.F. von (1856-67) Treatise on Physiological Optics.

Hess, EH (1975) "The role of pupil size in communication," Scientific American, 233(5), 110–12.

Heyes, C.M. (1998) Theory of mind in nonhuman primates. Behavioral and Brain Sciences 21, 101-48; with commentaries.

Heyes, C.M. and Galef, B.G. (eds) (1996) Social Learning in Animals: The Roots of Culture. San Diego, CA, Academic Press.

Hilgard, E.R. (1986) Divided Consciousness: Multiple Controls in Human Thought and Action. New York, Wiley.

Hilton, E.N., Lundberg, T.R. Transgender Women in the Female Category of Sport: Perspectives on Testosterone Suppression and Performance Advantage. Sports Med 51, 199–214 (2021).

Hitler, Adolf. Mein Kampf, 1925

Hodgson, R. (1891) A case of double consciousness. Proceedings of the Society for Psychical Research 7, 221-58.

Hofstadter, D.R. and Dennett, D.C. (eds) (1981) The Mind's I: Fantasies and Reflections on Self and Soul. London, Penguin.

Holland, J. (ed.) (2001) Ecstasy: The Complete Guide: A Comprehensive Look at the Risks and Benefits of MDMA. Rochester, VT, Park Street Press.

Holmes, D.S. (1987) The influence of meditation versus rest on physiological arousal. In M. West (ed.) The Psychology of Meditation. Oxford, Clarendon Press, 81-103.

Holmstrom, David. 1992, Christian Science Monitor

Holt, J. (1999) Blindsight in debates about qualia. Journal of Consciousness Studies 6(5), 54-71.

Holloway RL (1996) Evolution of the human brain. In: Lock A, Peters CR (eds) Handbook of human symbolic evolution. Oxford University Press, Oxford

Iacoboni M, Woods RP, Brass M, Bekkering H, Mazziotta JC, Rizzolatti G (1999) Cortical mechanisms of human imitation. Science 286: 2526–2528.

Iacoboni M, Koski LM, Brass M, Bekkering H, Woods RP, Dubeau MC, Mazziotta JC, Rizzolatti G (2001) Reafferent copies of imitated actions in the right superior temporal cortex. Proc Natl Acad Sci USA 98: 13995–13999.

Jeannerod M (1988) The neural and behavioural organization of goal-directed movements. Clarendon Press, Oxford.

Johnson-Frey SH, Maloof FR, Newman-Norlund R, Farrer C, Inati S, Grafton ST (2003) Actions or hand-objects interactions? Human inferior frontal cortex and action observation. Neuron 39: 1053–1058.

Jackson, F. (1982) Epiphenomenal qualia. Philosophical Quarterly 32, 127-36.

James, W. (1890) The Principles of Psychology (2 volumes). London, Macmillan.

James, W. (1902) The Varieties of Religious Experience: A Study in Human Nature. New York and London, Longmans, Green and Co.

Jansen, K. (2001) Ketamine: Dreams and Realities. Sarasota, FL, Multidisciplinary Association for Psychedelic Studies.

Jay, M. (ed.) (1999) Artificial Paradises: A Drugs Reader. London, Penguin.

Jaynes, J. (1976) The Origin of Consciousness in the Breakdown of the Bicameral Mind. New York, Houghton Mifflin.

Johnson, M.K. and Raye, C.L. (1981) Reality monitoring. Psychological Review 88, 67-85.

Kadim I, Mahgoub O, Baqir S et al. (2015) Cultured meat from muscle stem cells: a review of challenges and prospects. J Integr Agr 14: 222–233

Kandel, E. R. In Search of Memory: The Emergence of a New Science of Mind, W. W. Norton & Company (2007).

Kandel E. R. Schwartz JH, Jessel TM. Principles of neural sciences. New York; McGraw Hill, 2000.

Kanwisher, N. (2001) Neural events and perceptual awareness. Cognition

79, 89-113; also reprinted inS. Dehaene (ed.) The Cognitive Neuroscience of Consciousness. Cambridge, MA, MIT Press, 89-113.

Karn, K. and Hayhoe, M. (2000) Memory representations guide targeting eye movements in a natural task. Visual Cognition 7, 673-703.

Kennedy, H., & Dehay, C. (1988). Functional implications of the anatomical organization of the callosal projections of visual areas V1 and V2 in the macaque monkey. Behav. Brain Res., 29, 225–236.

Kentridge, R.W. and Heywood, C.A. (1999) The status of blindsight. Journal of Consciousness Studies 6(5), 3-11.

Kihlstrom, J.F. (1996) Perception without awareness of what is perceived, learning without awareness of what is learned. In M. Velmans (ed.) The Science of Consciousness. London, Routledge, 23-46.

Kosslyn, S.M. (1980) Image and Mind. Cambridge, MA, Harvard University Press.

Kosslyn, S.M. (1988) Aspects of a cognitive neuroscience of mental imagery. Science 240, 1621-6.

Kinsbourne, M. (1995), 'The intralaminar thalamic nucleii', Consciousness and Cognition, 4.

Kjaer, Troels, Camilla Bertelsen, Paola Piccini, David Brooks, Jorgen Alving, and Hans Lou. "Increased Dopamine Tone during Meditation- Induced Change of Consciousness." Cognitive Brain Research 13, no. 2 (April 2002)

Kölmel HW. 1985. Complex visual hallucinations in the hemianopic field. J Neurol Neurosurg Psychiatry.

Koenig, Harold. "Research on Religion, Spirituality, and Mental Health: A Review." Canadian Journal of Psychiatry 54, no. 5 (May 2009)

Koenig, Harold, ed. Handbook of Religion and Mental Health. San Diego, CA: Academic Press, 1998

Kraepelin E. Psychiatry: A Textbook for Students and Physicians. New York, NY: Science History Publications; 1990.

Lauglin, Charles, John McManus, and Eugene d'Aquili. Brain, Symbol, and Experience. 2nd ed. New York: Columbia University Press, 1992

Lakoff, G. and M. Johnson (1999). Philosophy in the flesh. Basic Books: New York.

LeDoux, J. E. (1996). The emotional brain. New York: Simon & Schuster.

LeDoux, J.E. (1992), 'Emotion and the amygdala', in The Amygdala: Neurobiological Aspects of Emo- tion, Memory and Mental Dysfunction, ed J.P. Aggleton (New York: Wiley-Liss).

Levin, D.T. and Simons, D.J. (1997) Failure to detect changes to attended objects in motion pictures. Psychonomic Bulletin and Review 4, 501-6.

Levine,J. (1983) Materialism and qualia: the explanatory gap. Pacific Philosophical Quarterly 64, 354-61.

Levine,J. (2001) Purple Haze: The Puzzle of Consciousness. New York, Oxford University Press. Levine, S. (1979) A Gradual Awakening. New York, Doubleday.

Levinson, B.W. (1965) States of awareness during general anaesthesia. British Journal of Anaesthesia 37, 544-6.

Lewicki, P., Czyzewska, M. and Hoffman, H. (1987) Unconscious acquisition of complex procedural knowledge. Journal of Experimental Psychology: Learning, Memory and Cognition 13, 523-30.

Lewicki, P., Hill, T. and Bizot, E. (1988) Acquisition of procedural knowledge about a pattern of stimuli that cannot be articulated. Cognitive Psychology 20, 24-37.

Lewicki, P., Hill, T. and Czyzewska, M. (1992) Nonconscious acquisition of information. American Psychologist 47, 796-801.

Manthey S, Schubotz RI, von Cramon DY (2003). Premotor cortex in observing erroneous action: an fMRI study. Brain Res Cogn Brain Res 15: 296–307.

Mesulam MM, Mufson EJ (1982) Insula of the old world monkey. III: Efferent cortical output and comments on function. J Comp Neurol 212: 38–52.

Naskar, Abhijit. "Homo: A Brief History of Consciousness", 2015

Naskar, Abhijit. "What is Mind?", 2016

Naskar, Abhijit. "Love, God & Neurons: Memoir of A Scientist who found himself by getting lost", 2016

Naskar, Abhijit. "Principia Humanitas", 2017

Naskar, Abhijit. "We Are All Black: A Treatise on Racism", 2017

Naskar, Abhijit. "Either Civilized or Phobic: A Treatise on Homosexuality", 2017

Naskar, Abhijit. "The Bengal Tigress: A Treatise on Gender Equality", 2017

Naskar, Abhijit. "Morality Absolute", 2017

Naskar, Abhijit. "Build Bridges not Walls: In the name of Americana", 2018

Naskar, Abhijit. "Fabric of Humanity", 2018

Naskar, Abhijit. "Citizens of Peace: Beyond the Savagery of Sovereignty", 2019

Naskar, Abhijit. "The Constitution of The United Peoples of Earth", 2019

Naskar, Abhijit. "Neurons Giveth, Neurons Taketh Away | Abhijit Naskar | TEDxIIMRanchi", 2019 https://www.youtube.com/watch?v=BNX-Q0ySm80

Naskar, Abhijit. "Mission Reality", 2019

Naskar, Abhijit. "Operation Justice: To Make A Society That Needs No Law", 2019

Naskar, Abhijit. "Every Generation Needs Caretakers: The Gospel of Patriotism", 2020

Naskar, Abhijit. "Hurricane Humans: Give me accountability, I'll give you peace", 2020

Naskar, Abhijit. "Revolution Indomable", 2020

Naskar, Abhijit. "Servitude is Sanctitude", 2020

Naskar, Abhijit. "Good Scientist: When Science and Service Combine", 2020

Newberg, Andrew, and Jeremy Iversen. "The Neural Basis of the Complex Mental Task of Meditation: Neurotransmitter and Neurochemical Considerations." Medical Hypotheses 61, no. 2 (2003).

Newberg, Andrew. "How God Changes Your Brain: An Introduction to Jewish Neurotheology", CCAR Journal: The Reform Jewish Quarterly, Winter 2016.

Newberg, Andrew, and Stephanie Newberg. "A Neuropsychological Perspective on Spiritual Development." In Handbook of Spiritual Development in Childhood and Adolescence, edited by Eugene

Roehlkepartain, Pamela King, Linda Wagener, and Peter Benson. London: Sage Publications, Inc., 2005

Newberg, Andrew. "The Neurotheology Link An Intersection Between Spirituality and Health", Alternative and Complimentary Therapies, Vol 21 No 1, February 2015.

Newberg, Andrew, Nancy Wintering, Dharma Khalsa, Hannah Roggenkamp, and Mark Waldman. "Meditation Effects on Cognitive Function and Cerebral Blood Flow in Subjects with Memory Loss: A Preliminary Study." Journal of Alzheimer's Disease 20, no. 2 (2010)

Nash, M. (1995), 'Glimpses of the mind', Time.

Nesse RM. Proximate and evolutionary studies of anxiety, stress and depression: synergy at the interface. Neurosci Biobehav Rev. 1999;23:895-903.

Nicolelis, Miguel. (2011) "Beyond Boundaries: The New Neuroscience of Connecting Brains with Machines---and How It Will Change Our Lives", Times Books

O'Hara, K. and Scutt, T. (1996) There is no hard problem of consciousness. Journal of Consciousness Studies 3(4), 290-302, reprinted in J. Shear (ed.) (1997) Explaining Consciousness. Cambridge, MA, MIT Press, 69-82.

O'Regan, J.K. (1992) Solving the "real" mysteries of visual perception: the world as an outside memory. Canadian Journal of Psychology 46, 461-88.

O'Regan, J.K. and Noe, A. (2001) A sensorimotor account of vision and visual consciousness. Behavioral and Brain Sciences 24(5), 883-917.

O'Regan, J.K., Rensink, R.A. and Clark,].]. (1999) Change-blindness as a result of "mudsplashes." Nature 398, 34.

Ornstein, R.E. (1977) The Psychology of Consciousness (2nd edn). New York, Harcourt.

Ornstein, R.E. (1986) The Psychology of Consciousness (3rd edn). New York, Pehguin.

Ornstein, R.E. (1992) The Evolution of Consciousness. New York, Touchstone.

Penfield W, Faulk ME (1955) The insula: further observations on its function. Brain 78: 445– 470.

Penrose, R. (1994), Shadows of the Mind (Oxford: Oxford University Press).

Penrose, R. (1989), The Emperor's New Mind: Concerning Computers, Minds and The Laws of Physics (Oxford: Oxford University Press).

Persinger, "'I would kill in God's name' role of sex, weekly church attendance, report of a religious experience and limbic lability" Perceptual and Motor Skills 1997.

Persinger "Experimental simulation of the God experience" Neurotheology 2003.

Persinger, Corradini, Clement, Keaney, et al "Neurotheology and its convergence with neuroquantology" NeuroQuantology 2010.

Persinger, Koren and St-Pierre "The electromagnetic induction of mystical and altered states within the laboratory" Journal of Consciousness Exploration and Research 2010.

Persinger "Case report: A prototypical spontaneous 'sensed presence' of a sentient being and concomitant electroencephalographic activity in the clinical laboratory" Neurocase 2008.

Persinger and Saroka "Potential production of Hughlings Jackson's "parasitic consciousness" by physiologically-patterned weak transcerebral magnetic fields: QEEG and source localization" Epilepsy & Behavior 28 (2013).

Persinger. "The neuropsychiatry of paranormal experiences". J Neuropsychiatry Clin Neurosci 2001.

Persinger. "Neuropsychological bases of god beliefs", New York: Praeger, 1987

Persinger. "Temporal lobe epileptic signs and correlative behaviors displayed by normal populations", Journal of General Psychology, 1986

Perry BD, Pollard R. Homeostasis, stress, trauma, and adaptation. A neurodevelopmental view of childhood trauma. Child Adolesc Psychiatr Clin N Am. 1998;7:33.

Paré, D. & Llinás, R. (1995), 'Conscious and preconscious processes as seen from the standpoint of sleep-waking cycle neurophysiology', Neuropsychologia, 33.

Phillips ML, Young AW, Senior C, Brammer M, Andrew C, Calder AJ, Bullmore ET, Perrett DI, Rowland D, Williams SC, Gray JA, David AS (1997) A specific neural substrate for perceiving facial expressions of disgust. Nature 389: 495–498.

Phillips ML, Young AW, Scott SK, Calder AJ, Andrew C, Giampietro V, Williams SC, Bullmore ET, Brammer M, Gray JA (1998) Neural responses to facial and vocal expressions of fear and disgust. Proc R Soc Lond B Biol Sci 265: 1809–1817.

Puce A, Perrett D (2003) Electrophysiological and brain imaging of biological motion. Philosoph Trans Royal Soc Lond, Series B, 358: 435–445.

Ramachandran VS. Behavioral and magnetoencephalographic correlates of plasticity in the adult human brain. Proc Natl Acad Sci USA 1993; 90: 10413–20.

Ramachandran VS. Phantom limbs, neglect syndromes, repressed memories, and Freudian psychology. Int Rev Neurobiol 1994; 37: 291–333.

Ramachandran VS. Plasticity and functional recovery in neurology. Clin Med 2005; 5: 368–73.

Ramachandran VS, Hirstein W. The perception of phantom limbs. The D. O. Hebb lecture. Brain 1998; 121: 1603–30.

Ramachandran VS, Rogers-Ramachandran D, Cobb S. Touching the phantom limb. Nature 1995; 377: 489–90.

Ramachandran VS, Rogers-Ramachandran D. Phantom limbs and

neural plasticity. Arch Neurol 2000; 57: 317–20.

Ramachandran VS, Rogers-Ramachandran D. It's all done with mirrors. Sci Am Mind 2007; 18: 16–9.

Ramachandran VS, Rogers-Ramachandran D. Sensations referred to a patient's phantom arm from another subjects intact arm: perceptual correlates of mirror neurons. Med Hypotheses 2008; 70: 1233–4.

Ramachandran VS, Rogers-Ramachandran D, Stewart M. Perceptual correlates of massive cortical reorganization. Science 1992; 258: 1159–60.

Rizzolatti G, Craighero L (2004) The mirror-neuron system. Annu Rev Neurosci 27: 169–192.

Rizzolatti G, Fogassi L, Gallese V (2001) Neurophysiological mechanisms underlying the understanding and imitation of action. Nature Rev Neurosci 2:661–670.

Rock I, Victor J. Vision and touch: an experimentally created conflict between the two senses. Science 1964; 143: 594–6.

Rose´n B, Lundborg G. Training with a mirror in rehabilitation of the hand. Scand J Plast Reconstr Surg Hand Surg 2005; 39: 104–8.

Roberts, TA; Smalley, J; Ahrendt, D (December 2020). "Effect of gender affirming hormones on athletic performance in transwomen and transmen: implications for sporting organisations and legislators". British Journal of Sports Medicine. 55 (11): 577–583

Royet JP, Plailly J, Delon-Martin C, Kareken DA, Segebarth C (2003) fMRI of emotional responses to odors: influence of hedonic valence and judgment, handedness, and gender. Neuroimage 20: 713–728.

Rozin R Haidt J and McCauley CR (2000) Disgust. In: Lewis M, Haviland-Jones JM (eds) Handbook of Emotion. 2nd Edition. Guilford Press, New York, pp 637–653.

Saxe R, Carey S, Kanwisher N (2004) Understanding other minds: linking developmental psychology and functional neuroimaging. Annu Rev Psychol 55: 87–124.

S. J. Russell and P. Norvig, Artificial intelligence: a modern approach (3rd edition): Prentice Hall, 2009.

Singer T, Seymour B, O'Doherty J, Kaube H, Dolan RJ, Frith CD (2004) Empathy for pain involves the affective but not the sensory components of pain. Science 303: 1157–1162.

Smith A (1759) The theory of moral sentiments (ed. 1976). Clarendon Press, Oxford.

Schilling, Vincent. 2017, indian country today

Stein, Stephen K. 2017, The Sea in World History: Exploration, Travel, and Trade

Simonsen R (2015) Eating for the future: veganism and the challenge of in vitro meat. In: Stapleton P, Byers A (Hg). Biopolitics and utopia. Palgrave Macmillan, New York (2015), S 167–190

Tesla N. "My Inventions", 1919

T. R. Society, "Machine learning: the power and promise of computers that learn by example," ed. The Royal Society, 2017.

Tomasello M, Call J (1997) Primate cognition. Oxford University Press, Oxford.

EITHER REFORMIST OR TERRORIST